Can W
Imagine
a Future
Together?

INTERCULTURAL LESSONS FOR
LIVING IN LOVE AND FAITH

MARTYN SNOW

CHURCH HOUSE
PUBLISHING

Contents

Introduction **Living in Love and Faith**   5

Chapter 1   **A season of discernment**   19

Chapter 2   **Interculturalism and gift exchange**   29

Chapter 3   **Interculturalism and gift exchange
             applied to LLF**   43

Chapter 4   **A love letter to the church**   57

Further resources   64

INTRODUCTION

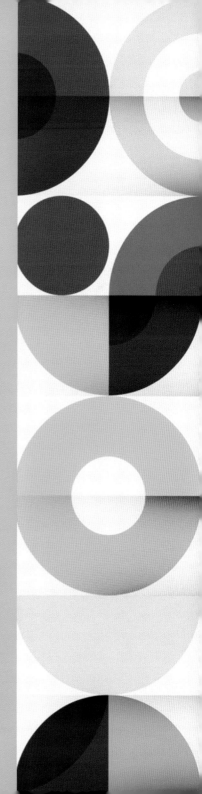

Recently, a friend recommended to me the TV programme *Couples Therapy*. This fly-on-the-wall documentary follows a therapist as she meets with various couples (both opposite- and same-sex). Over a period of months, we watch as the therapist helps each couple to listen to one another, build a deeper understanding of themselves and their relationship, and together imagine a new future. Sometimes that future involves re-committing to one another and going deeper in their relationship. Sometimes it is about separation.

Of course, the therapist can't make the decision for the couple – they must decide for themselves. But the therapist is skilled at getting both parties to tell their stories. She then helps them to reflect on their feelings and uncover what lies behind their behaviour.

Often, each party will express how they are torn. Part of them wants to shout and scream as their emotions get the better of them, and part of them wants to embrace the other and get back to how things were. Sometimes they acknowledge that their own pain is making it very hard to truly listen to the other. And it is common for them to voice very different understandings of the history of the conflict, the nature of the conflict, and the question of who should act first to de-escalate the conflict.

I am not suggesting that there is a direct equivalence between couples therapy and Living in Love and Faith! Yet as a church we are deeply divided over questions of identity, sexuality and marriage. And I detect levels of pain in the

Church of England which are making it very difficult for us to go on listening to one another.

Living in Love and Faith (LLF) has been running for a long time (officially since 2017, but unofficially much longer). Many hurtful things have been said and done during that period and for some, it is hard to see a way back. Can we go on living together in one church, or is now the moment of separation? And if we are to stay together, will we be living separate lives in separate rooms, or can we remain soulmates?

These are the questions at the heart of this booklet.

Like the therapist, I cannot decide the answer to these questions. I cannot compel people to imagine a future together if that is not what they want. But given the hours that I have spent trying to listen to different parties and the hours spent trying to steer the process, I have come to a view which I hope offers some inspiration for a possible way forward together.

That view can be summarised as:

1. We've not yet reached the point of separation – or even living in separate rooms.
2. So, we are in a season of discernment. Given our profound disagreements, can we imagine a new future together?
3. This season will require prayer, listening, and practical acts of kindness as we re-imagine how we serve a divided society and proclaim the Good News.

4.   There are models available to us from other fields which might help us re-imagine. One is called 'interculturalism' and the other 'gift exchange'. This booklet is an attempt to set out how they might help.

As a reader, you may disagree with what you have already read! And you may have your own view about how our situation could be changed. Unfortunately, unlike with a therapist, we can't have a genuine dialogue about this – the written word doesn't allow for that (although there has been a lot of good dialogue as part of the LLF process).

So, I can only apologise now, if I misrepresent your views or if you feel that I am being unfair in summarising different positions. But my prayer is that you will read what follows in the spirit it is intended, which is a sincere appreciation for the whole Church of England and a heartfelt desire for us to thrive as one church and model God's ministry of reconciliation to a divided world.

What is Living in Love and Faith?

Living in Love and Faith (LLF) is a process that has been under way since 2017 to help the church in its discernment on matters of identity, sexuality, relationships and marriage.[1] The views of many in society have changed rapidly in the last few decades – civil partnerships were introduced in 2005, and same-sex marriages were legalised in 2014. So, the church has sought to respond.

LLF started when the House of Bishops brought a paper on marriage and same-sex relationships to General Synod in February 2017.[2] There had already been a series of 'shared conversations' seeking dialogue across our differences. Nevertheless, General Synod rejected the House of Bishops' paper. The then Archbishop of Canterbury, Justin Welby, responded to the Synod's decision by stating:

No person is a problem, or an issue. People are made in the image of God. All of us, without exception, are loved and called in Christ. There are no 'problems', there are simply people.

How we deal with the real and profound disagreement – put so passionately and so clearly by many at the Church of England's General Synod debate on marriage and same-sex relationships today – is the challenge we face as people who all belong to Christ.

To deal with that disagreement, to find ways forward, we need a radical new Christian inclusion in the Church. This must be founded in scripture, in reason, in tradition, in theology; it must be based on good, healthy, flourishing relationships, and in a proper 21st-century understanding of being human and of being sexual.

We need to work together – not just the bishops but the whole Church, not excluding anyone – to move forward with confidence.

The vote today is not the end of the story, nor was it intended to be. As bishops we will think again and go on

thinking, and we will seek to do better. We could hardly
fail to do so in the light of what was said this afternoon.

The way forward needs to be about love, joy and
celebration of our humanity; of our creation in the image
of God, of our belonging to Christ – all of us, without
exception, without exclusion.[3]

This powerful statement, led to the formation of a number of
working groups tasked with examining the Bible, theology,
history, and social and biological sciences. A suite of resources
was produced in 2020, at the heart of which was a 'learning hub',
a book and a training course.[4] Underlying all of this were agreed
'Pastoral Principles' aimed at ensuring good dialogue.[5] And then
a large-scale listening exercise was conducted with over 6,000
people from across the church.[6]

Eventually, in February 2023, General Synod voted to
allow Prayers of Love and Faith (PLF) to be used with same-
sex couples in existing services (and soon in bespoke services).[7]
These prayers are not a form of marriage service, nor do they
equate the relationships brought before God to marriage, but
they do seek to celebrate God's gifts and grace in other forms
of committed, faithful relationships, and to ask for God's guidance
and blessing as the couple seek to grow in love and faith.

More generally, in 2023, the House of Bishops issued
an apology for a failure to welcome LGBTQI+ (lesbian, gay,
bisexual, transgender, queer, intersex) people and committed
itself to address this lack of welcome and inclusion. Different
dioceses have approached the work of apology in contrasting

ways. Some have introduced LGBTQI+ chaplains, and bishops actively participate in 'Pride' events and 'Open Table Network'. In other dioceses, it has been left up to individual parishes to sign up to 'Inclusive Church' or other similar networks. Many Cathedrals have also played a significant role in welcoming and including LGBTQI+ people. And an umbrella group, 'Together for the Church of England'[8] has emerged with the aim of 'full inclusion and equality'.

Yet at the same time, a network of organisations known as 'The Alliance' has arisen which sees the development of Prayers of Love of Faith as indicative of a change in the church's historic doctrine of marriage.[9] Members of The Alliance are deeply unhappy with the process behind the introduction of PLF, the perceived departure from historic and biblical teaching, and the break with the position of ecumenical partner churches and many Provinces of the Anglican Communion in the Global South. They have pushed for 'pastoral provision' for those clergy and churches who cannot in conscience use the PLF, arguing that they should be allowed their own bishops and potentially even their own Province i.e. their own Archbishop.

At the time of writing (Autumn 2024) the House of Bishops has resisted this level of provision, preferring instead to offer a form of 'delegated episcopal ministry' (DEM) for these churches, i.e. another bishop but one who is still under the legal jurisdiction of the diocesan bishop.

Further questions remain to be addressed in the LLF process. Can clergy and lay ministers be permitted to enter same-sex civil marriages? (Currently they may not.) What is the appropriate context for sexual intimacy? When might the church allow same-sex marriages to happen in our buildings?

And then there are wider questions of identity and relationships. The church – like wider society – is struggling to know how to support and include transgender people, as well as single people, blended families and those who have been adopted. And, as numbers of couples getting married continue to decline, what further effects might this have on society?

Finally, it is important to return to the first point made by Archbishop Justin in his 2017 speech. LLF is not a problem to be solved nor an issue to be addressed. Neither is it simply a debate about theology (though that is an important part of it). Rather this is about real people, and it is incredibly personal for many people, touching on their sense of identity and the deep-seated roots of sexuality. At times, we have fallen into hurtful language which has lost sight of the people most affected by the process. This has had tragic consequences, with reports of individuals self-harming and even taking their own lives.

Above all else, then, my hope for this booklet is that it will change the tone of our conversations. LLF has been and continues to be a painful process for all involved. And when we are hurt, we find it very hard to listen, and very hard to resist lashing out at others. This is a perfectly natural response. Yet this is not our calling as Christians. So how do we live as disciples of Jesus Christ when we disagree so profoundly, and we are part of a fractured church?

Who am I and in what capacity am I writing?

Unlike the therapist referred to above, I cannot claim to be neutral on this topic. I have my own hopes and concerns. So, it is only right that I say a little about my own position and background.

First and foremost, I am a disciple of Jesus Christ who is hungry to learn and grow in my faith. Several generations of my family have been missionaries, and my background lies within a conservative Christian tradition which places a very high value on the Bible, on holiness and on the urgency of sharing the gospel of Jesus Christ. Yet I have also had the privilege of learning from different traditions and cultures around the world. This has thrown up new questions and perspectives. Hence, I see myself primarily as a missionary bishop shaped by the world church.

Secondly, I am a white, heterosexual male which means it is very difficult for me to understand so much of what LGBTQI+ people experience in their lives. I am also a bishop in the Church of England, a role which carries a degree of power. Every time I meet with LGBTQI+ people, or with clergy and lay people opposed to the use of PLF, there is a power dynamic which is not always easy to articulate but it governs what is and what isn't said, how it is said and how it is received. I do my best to acknowledge this, but it is complex, and I know that I often get it wrong.

Thirdly, while many would view me as 'conservative' on the question of marriage, holding to a traditional understanding of marriage as a lifelong union of one man and one woman, I am keenly aware of the hurt and pain that I and others in the church have caused to LGBTQI+ people. We have been far too ready to judge, to 'other' and to exclude, and we must repent of this sin. Of course, many will feel that such repentance involves opening up marriage to same-sex couples, but I am personally struggling to square that with Scripture. I understand that some will see this as inconsistent, but it is probably not the only area of inconsistency in my beliefs and practices!

Finally, I am determined to work for a church which includes people who don't just have a different view, but also a different practice of holy living, in the hope that we can learn from one another (hence this booklet, and hence my willingness to take on the role of Lead Bishop for LLF). I see much that is good in the lives of people with whom I disagree, so I choose to focus on the good – in the hope that they too will give me the benefit of the doubt. This is not a simplistic plea to 'agree to disagree' on these questions, but rather a plea to re-imagine the future of the Church of England given our shared desire to 'proclaim afresh in this generation' the Good News of Jesus Christ and given the urgency of this task in a world of profound and increasingly violent divisions.[10]

Outline of this booklet

It was shortly after writing the book *An Intercultural Church for a Multicultural World: Reflections on Gift Exchange* (Church House Publishing, 2024), that I was asked by the archbishops to be Lead Bishop for the LLF process. The concept of interculturalism was therefore at the forefront of my mind and has shaped much of my thinking about this phase of the LLF work. My thinking on interculturalism arose from work we have done in the Diocese of Leicester, after recognising that despite the cultural diversity of our city, our worshipping communities were largely homogenous, and church leaders did not feel confident in navigating cultural differences. We have sought to explore how we can live together well across difference such that all members of our churches, especially those who have been historically marginalised, flourish and we can better witness together to the God of all nations.

Again, I am not suggesting a direct equivalence between cultural/ethnic differences and sexuality.[11] They have some things in common but also some things which are unique. But questions of living well together across difference are important for our society, the church as a whole and for congregations, where worshippers, staff teams and PCCs may disagree on questions of sexuality.

So, the first chapter of this booklet offers a brief overview of complexities of our disagreement over LLF. There are multiple questions within LLF, none of which are likely to be resolved anytime soon. Indeed, I believe we should stop looking for 'technical fixes' (to quote the leadership writer Ronald Heifetz) and instead see the need for 'adaptive change' (addressing the need to learn how to live well with differences).[12] Hence my argument that we are still in a 'season of discernment', seeking to imagine a new future together. This discernment is not only on the matter of same-sex relationships but also on the future shape of the Church of England.

To help us in this discernment, I am suggesting approaching the questions of LLF from a very different angle. Chapter 3 starts by exploring the broad concept of culture and then introduces the terms interculturalism and gift exchange. And there are plenty of questions for reflection, which I hope will stimulate your own thinking in this area before, in Chapter 4, I suggest how it may apply to LLF. My plea is for a shift of focus from fixing our disagreements to 'habits' and 'attitudes' which allow us to live well together.

I fully understand that some readers will disagree with me. If LLF is about a fundamental theological disagreement which is so profound that proponents of both views must separate or live in separate rooms, then concepts like interculturalism and gift exchange will be of little value (or more specifically, they will be an ecumenical or interfaith endeavour like 'receptive ecumenism').[13] Or, if LLF is about righting a severe injustice, then it might be thought that I am arguing for oppressor and oppressed to be reconciled and live together in a way which risks perpetuating injustice.

However, it is my own sense that there is a third group of people in the Church of England (rarely heard from) who do not see LLF in either of these terms. So rather than simply trying to force our views on others, can we not focus for a season on maintaining the relationships and practising gift exchange so that we all grow in our discipleship?

Each chapter in this booklet contains some questions for reflection. These would be best explored in small groups, although they could also resource individual learning. But I hope there is enough within this booklet to provide resources for three or four evenings of small group prayer, reflection and discussion.

At the end of the booklet, I have put some suggestions for other resources which could be used alongside this booklet. But as a minimum, any group using this booklet should remind themselves of the 'Pastoral Principles' produced by the Church of England.[14] These will help to ensure the group is a 'safe space' for everyone involved.[15]

My final chapter is a love letter to the church. (As I am not a couples' therapist, I think I am entitled to write a love letter!) Yet, I am still cautious about offering a solution, or even a long-term peace plan. My 'seasonal' approach will seem unsatisfactory to many. I am regularly asked about the endpoint or goal of LLF, and I honestly can't give an answer to this. The established status of the Church of England makes us unlike any other province of the Anglican Communion and adds layers of complexity. And even if we could be sure of the endpoint, we would need to consider carefully how to get there (the end doesn't always justify the means).

So, my plea is that we recommit to learning, to discipleship and the way of love.

1. A SEASON OF DISCERNMENT

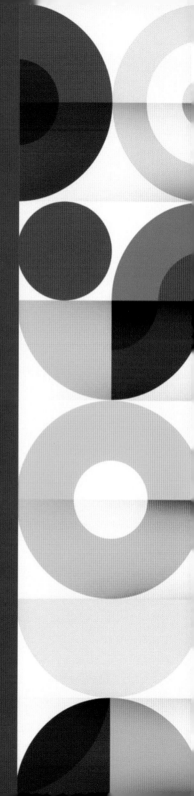

Ron Heifetz in his 1994 provocatively-titled book *Leadership without Easy Answers* describes the difference between technical work and adaptive work. Technical work is the application of known solutions to known problems. But what if our situation is not a problem but instead a changed environment? What if our situation – to use a topical analogy – is not simply that we have a leaky washing machine which has flooded the kitchen (and which could easily be fixed) but that the house has flooded because of the amount of rain caused by climate change (something which cannot be fixed without a significant shift in the thinking of most of the population). What if we have a condition which requires adaptive work rather than a technical fix?

Could it be that our disagreements in the church are something that we must learn to live with? Could it be that our disagreements are a condition which is not going to change in our lifetimes? It could even be argued that such disagreements are built into Anglicanism – we were born in dispute with Rome, our early history involved much bloodshed, the 'ejection' of ministers who refused to use The Book of Common Prayer and recognise the authority of bishops, and multiple other controversies. This is arguably the greatest challenge and greatest gift of Anglicanism.

So, what does it mean to 'learn to live with this condition'? Heifetz suggests it's about learning – accepting that we don't have the answers, and we often make mistakes, yet committing to go on learning. This is part of the reason why I have rejected calls to pause or stop the LLF process even though we are deeply divided (some motions in Synod have been passed by margins of one or two votes), and even though the current safeguarding crisis is causing us to rethink much of what we are doing. Adaptive change is about learning, and this is now more important than ever.

This is also why I have resisted calls to go back to the beginning of the process, even though the process itself has been highly contested. Calls to start again with a Canon B 2 Synodical process (the formal process for changing 'forms of service' which requires a two-thirds majority in General Synod) or calls to start again with a proposal to move immediately to equal marriage are, in my view, attempts at technical fixes. Even if we were to do this, the disagreements would not go away, and the challenge to learn to live with the disagreements would still remain (as we are finding with the 1994 and 2014 'settlements' over the ordination of women).

So, maybe the next stage of our learning is about Christian discipleship in a divided world. In a culture which increasingly seeks to resolve disputes by resorting to legal action (numbers of lawyers in the USA rose from 326,000 in 1970 to 1.3 million in 2000)[16] and a culture which is increasingly fragmented (20 million people watched the Morecombe and Wise Christmas show in 1977, whereas in 2023 the most watched TV programme on Christmas Day was the King's message with 5 million viewers), the church has to adapt and learn. And I believe that the core of this learning is about practical acts of kindness and generosity towards those with whom we disagree – unsurprisingly taking us back to the one we claim to follow – Jesus Christ. In this way, even while our differences remain on show for all the world to see, we continue to witness to the one who said, 'by this everyone will know that you are my disciples, if you love one another' (John 13.35).

I said in the Introduction that my own view is that we've not yet reached a point of separation, or of having to live in separate rooms. Of course, some people have left the Church of England already. Some LGBTQI+ people have left to join other denominations (and sadly, some have left church altogether). And some who are unhappy about LLF have left to join networks such as the Anglican Mission in Europe. As yet, however, the numbers are relatively small, and we haven't reached the point of large-scale departures. At the same time, I often hear from people in different positions on LLF that they are committed and want to stay in the Church of England, even as we wrestle with differing hopes and visions for our church. So in my view, we are still in a season of discernment – a season of imagining a new future together.

That word – discernment – has been used a lot in the LLF process, yet often without real understanding of its meaning. A recent review of the process of appointing bishops had this to say about discernment:

> 'Discernment' is a word used in English translations of the bible for two common Greek verbs, one of which,

diakrinein, describes the act of distinguishing things that are not easy to distinguish, especially spiritual and moral alternatives that demand a spiritual insight. The other, dokimazein, has the sense of 'examining' and 'approving', and is often used of future courses of action: we are to discern 'what is pleasing to the Lord' (Ephesians 5.10), 'what is the will of God' (Romans 12.2) ... What is indicated by this range of senses is, above all, a kind of insight ... Discernment involves a step of faith enabling us to conceive something that God will bring about, which is not yet objectively visible.[17]

So LLF is intended to be a prayerful process of discerning 'what is pleasing to the Lord' in a world where our understanding of biology, anthropology and sociology have grown significantly. This is not a simple process – and neither is it a simple binary, i.e. some believe the Bible, and others believe in science. Everyone I know in the Church of England believes in both. But it is true to say that there are differences of emphasis.

For instance, the recently published book *The Widening of God's Mercy: Sexuality Within the Biblical Story* by Christopher and Richard Hays (Yale University Press, 2024), recounts the change in understanding of these two authors (father and son – both biblical scholars). In their earlier works, they focused on specific verses in the Bible which appear clear in their condemnation of homosexual practice. Now they look to the larger narrative of the Bible, which (they argue) is all about God's mercy being widened to include more and more people.

Of course, not everyone agrees with this approach – in their reviews of the book, both Andrew Goddard[18] and Martin Davie,[19] argue that the Hays' account sounds like today's progressive political agenda being read back into the Bible.

Yet alongside these questions of biblical interpretation and morality, we are also discerning other areas. Significantly, we are also discerning the future shape of the Church of England.

In times past, everyone who lived in England was regarded as part of the Church of England, and every church was expected to conform to national expectations in terms of liturgy and pastoral practice. Arguably, this began to fracture following the 1927 Prayer Book Crisis, when the House of Commons voted not to approve a revision of the The Book of Common Prayer (1662) that had been twenty years in the making. The century that followed has seen ever greater variety in styles of worship, approaches to mission and understandings of what it means to be the established church of the land. So the roots of the disagreement around LLF do not lie solely in questions of theology and morality. They also relate to ecclesiology (understandings of the church), and other linked questions such as the relationship between the local church and the national, and the interplay between individual and collective conscience (a major part of the Reformation split).

Then there is the question of mission. What does it mean to be the established church of the land in a society where fewer and fewer people call themselves Christian (46% in the last census, down from 71% in 2001)? Should our priority be presence (serving every person in every parish) – or evangelism and the call to repentance and belief?

In stating the question this starkly, I know some readers will be exasperated – surely, we can do both? Yet the argument has been used repeatedly in the LLF debate that the church will only grow if we adopt one approach or the other (with evidence from other countries or other institutions produced to back up the case). Personally, I don't think the growth of the church is linked to any one factor (other than the action of God!). Rather, the specifics of our context play a large part in deciding the health of the soil in which the seed of the gospel is planted. And our context is changing rapidly – not least in terms of demographics. (My own city of Leicester now has a population with more than 50% of people of Global Majority Heritage.)

So, for all these reasons, I am advocating a seasonal approach. We will not settle the multiple disputes within LLF anytime soon – indeed, I doubt any of them will be settled within my lifetime. So, the key question is what is needed for this next season in the life of the church? Can we imagine a new future together? In all our brokenness and dysfunctionality, can we draw on the riches of the Bible, our history and tradition, and imagine a new future where we are kind and considerate to one another, loving and generous – witnessing as one body to the resurrection life of our Lord Jesus Christ?

I want now to look at these questions from a very different angle. As mentioned in the introduction, I want to explore whether there are lessons to learn from our cultural diversity and how we have responded to this. There is no direct equivalence with LLF – culture and sexuality have some things in common, and some aspects which are very different. Nevertheless, our society cannot agree about immigration and integration. And cultural diversity is complex and multi-layered. It evokes strong feelings. And it is an area explored in the Bible through stories of migration and hospitality, and images of diversity and unity such as the body of Christ.

So let me start by exploring the broad concept of culture and then introduce the terms interculturalism and gift exchange. And then in the following chapter, I will explore how they might apply to LLF.

Questions for reflection

1. If there are no easy answers to our disagreements, how might 'learning to live with this condition' help shape our understanding and actions?

2. Many people feel angry, disappointed and upset about this area of disagreement. How do you feel? It may be helpful to acknowledge to God the reality of your feelings (as the Psalmist often does).

3. Can you think of times when you have had to 'discern what is pleasing to the Lord'? What has helped you in this process of discernment?

4. If we are discerning the future shape of the Church of England, what are the core elements which need to remain unchanged, and what are the elements which might need to be adapted?

2. INTERCULTURALISM AND GIFT EXCHANGE

It could be argued that the Bible is a story of migration. From Adam and Eve being expelled from the Garden, to Abraham, who sets out with his family to a new land, to the Exodus and onto the Exile. Most of the Old Testament is written in a context of migration (with plenty of warnings about what happens when we get too settled!).

Then there is the incarnation – God crossing borders to enter our world and 'pitching his tent among us' (one translation of John 1.14, more commonly read as 'the Word became flesh and dwelt among us'). Then the persecution and scattering of the Jerusalem church and the missionary journeys of Paul and others, and John receiving his revelation on the island of Patmos.

And so to our present day, where migration continues to shape the church as well as society. Vibrant churches in Nigeria are sending missionaries to the UK to establish new churches. Refugees from Ukraine bring their Orthodox faith and customs. And students from India and China are also enriching our churches.

Migration involves interaction between people of different cultures, and it is this that I want to explore in this chapter. Of course, there are many complexities to this, but I want to argue that in the Bible, the most significant response to migration is the instruction to 'welcome the stranger … for you were strangers in the land of Egypt' (Leviticus 19.34). Principally, this involves offering (and receiving) hospitality – something which was and is inbuilt to many cultures – but has sadly been lost in much of the Western world. And hospitality in turn, is an example of gift exchange between host and guest. But before I get there, let me step back and explore the following questions: what is culture? And how do cultures interact?

What is culture?

Culture is a complex term and used in a variety of ways. Sometimes we speak of a 'cultured' person – meaning someone who is well-educated and appreciates the arts! (Not a helpful understanding of the word.) Sometimes we speak of culture in evolutionary terms: 'advanced cultures' are those which have shed superstition and adopted a modern, rational, liberal approach to society (code for 'Western culture is superior to every other culture!').

However, more recently, an understanding has emerged of culture as the unspoken assumptions, beliefs and values behind our actions and words. Some would define it as 'the way we do things round here'. And in addition, an understanding has emerged that culture is fluid – constantly changing as we come into contact with people of other cultures – and contested – constantly being questioned regarding unspoken assumptions about power and meaning.

Some have also advanced the notion of hybrid cultures, to describe (for instance) the way a child may grow up in a family with roots in one culture, while living in a different culture – they are shaped by both cultures to some degree. Yet the notion has wider application. I may be primarily shaped by 'English culture' (however that is defined), yet I have also been shaped by the culture of the Church of England (an institution with a very strong culture of its own), and I may even have been shaped by a particular sub-culture of the Church of England, sometimes referred to as 'my tribe'. So there's an interesting question as to which one of these different cultures has been most significant in making me the person that I am?

Emmanuel Katongole is professor of Theology and Peace Studies at the University of Notre Dame in USA. He is the son of a Hutu mother and Tutsi father, and among his many books is one entitled: *Mirror to the Church: Resurrecting Faith after Genocide in Rwanda* (Zondervan, 2009). When asked the question: 'Is the blood of tribalism deeper than the waters of baptism?', Katongole surprised his American audience by saying:

> although Americans think of themselves as modern people, we might be affected by deeper forms of tribalism than we realize. Our circle of friends and the media we read and watch and listen to are prisms through which people see the world and know who are our friends and who are our enemies. We think [relying on] these prisms is the way God made us. But in the gospel, as I read it, there is a new creation, and we need to look through a new lens. The problem with racism and tribalism is they don't allow us to look through the new lens.

Katongole's books are full of stories of encounter. People of different tribes, people who were once enemies, people who feel they share little in common starting out on a journey towards another person, and in the process finding peace and discovering God's new creation. His central argument is that personal encounter is the only way to reconciliation – that's why the incarnation (God coming to meet with us) is so important for Christians.

Questions for reflection

1. What cultures have shaped you over the course of your life?

2. Do you see yourself as part of a sub-culture within the Church of England?

3. What contact do you have with people of other sub-cultures/tribes within the church?

Individual responses to other cultures

A lot of studies have been done on what happens when a person of one culture encounters a different culture. If you've ever lived abroad, at least some of this will be very familiar to you.

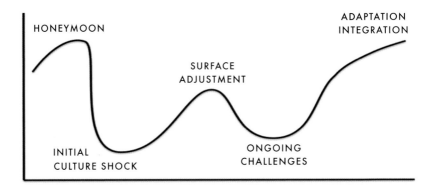

The different stages on this journey can be described as:[20]

1. Honeymoon – it's different, it's wonderful!

2. Distress – it's different, I can't cope!

3. Confrontation – it's different, it's wrong!

4. Surface adjustment – it's different, but I can function.

5. Deeper confrontation – I still don't understand why.

6. Deeper adjustment – I'm starting to understand why.

7. Adaption – the new normal.

Of course, there are complexities to this. We may react against certain parts of the new culture e.g. the place of women in society, or the treatment of Disabled people, and wrestle with the issue of whether this is simply a different way of doing things or whether this is genuinely evil and an infringement of universal human rights. In making this judgement call, it is important to acknowledge our own cultural bias (we all think our way of doing things is superior to other ways of doing things!) and to understand particular behaviours within the context of a different worldview. And for Christians this is a process of discernment – examining and approving 'what is pleasing to the Lord'.

Questions for reflection

1. Think about a time you've experienced a different culture – either by visiting a different country or encountering someone of a different background – does the journey outlined above ring true?

2. When you hit a moment of confrontation (this is different, and it can't be good) – what shaped your reaction? What presuppositions did you have?

3. If you managed to journey beyond the moment of confrontation, what helped you on that journey?

Societal responses to other cultures

Alongside this research on what happens when individuals of different cultures encounter one another, there is also a whole body of literature on what happens within societies. This falls broadly under the heading of integration i.e. how do people of different cultures integrate into the host / dominant culture.

- **Assimilation** – the people of the dominant culture send out strong signals to those of minority cultures that they must leave their own culture behind and adopt the dominant culture.

- **Multiculturalism** – all cultures are celebrated equally. The dominant culture is not imposed on others, rather we exist alongside each other and celebrate our differences.

- **Interculturalism** – recognises cultural differences **and** encourages interaction between people of different cultures.

So interculturalism is something of a reaction to assimilation – the forced imposition of one culture on people of another culture (which happens in the church as well as society). Interculturalism pays attention to power – how is the dominant culture interacting with minority cultures? What presuppositions do those of the dominant culture have ('we're superior', 'we're pure', 'others need to learn from us')? And how do those of minority cultures pick up on these signals? Sometimes it's very obvious – as in the language used in the press or on social media. Sometimes it can be very subtle – as in the imagery used in publicity, or the everyday rituals of greeting people.

Interculturalism is also something of a development of multiculturalism – the celebration of different cultures. This celebration is good, but it can have the unintended consequence of allowing people to live parallel lives, or, worse still, to live in ghettos. We all find it easiest to be with people 'like me'. So interculturalism seeks to encourage healthy encounters between people of different cultures. This is about more than simply bringing people together in one place. As we've seen, when individuals of different cultures encounter one another, there is a journey of adaption. So too, at a societal level, there is a journey of learning (particularly for Westerners like me who have a history of imposing our culture on others). This has sometimes been described as a continuum of cultural competence. We all start in different places on this continuum and move from one stage to another as our understanding and experience of different cultures grow.

- **Cultural destructiveness** – forced assimilation.

- **Cultural incompetence** – racism, prejudice, stereotypes.

- **Cultural ignorance** – differences ignored, 'treat everyone the same' (sounds good, but in reality, it perpetuates injustice).

- **Cultural pre-competence** – awareness of issues of culture but unsure of how to interact with people of a different culture.

- **Cultural competence** – exploring cultural differences through curiosity, dialogue and gift exchange.

- **Cultural proficiency** – actively implementing changes (in society or in church) to enable healthy interaction and mutual learning.

Questions for reflection

1. Where would you place yourself on this journey of learning about cultural competence? Be honest – you may not have had much contact with different cultures and that's fine. But you may have had more contact than you realise, hence the next question.

2. Given that the cultures and sub-cultures which have shaped us are about more than our place of birth or what ethnicity we regard ourselves, where are the places that you interact with people of different age groups, or people with different political views or people with a different worldview?

3. Given that interculturalism seeks to acknowledge different cultures and engage across cultures, can you think of examples of how you have learnt from people of a different culture?

What is gift exchange?

As I mentioned at the start of this chapter, the Bible gives lots of examples of people of different cultures encountering one another. We might think of the story of Ruth in the Old Testament – Ruth is a foreigner and widow who is welcomed into an Israelite family and cared for in a beautiful way. Or we might think of Peter and Cornelius in the book of Acts – their encounter leads to both of them being 'converted'. These, and many other stories, are examples of hospitality – the offering of food and shelter in a way which leads to friendship and community. So one model for the interaction of people of different cultures is gift exchange – each person brings gifts to share with the other. There is a mutual giving and receiving which can enrich both parties.

In my previous book (*An Intercultural Church for a Multicultural World*), I tell the story of discovering in West Africa the wide variety of gifts that can be shared. One was the gift of time, given to me by a woman who wanted to welcome me to the community but was too poor to bring a physical gift. So she gave me the gift of her time – sitting with me in silence.

The lesson was to come in handy for me, when sometime later, I visited a family who had just suffered a bereavement. I discovered that it was normal for the bereaved family to spend around a week sat in their house simply receiving visitors. And what a relief it was to discover that the visitors didn't need to say much, if anything at all. They simply sat with the family in silence. Silence too can be a gift (in the right context).

So, gifts come in all sorts of shapes and sizes. In white British, middle-class culture, we tend to think of the birthday and Christmas variety, or maybe the flowers and bottle of wine we take when going for dinner at a friend's house. But we also recognise the gift that an artist or musician 'possesses'. We call it a gift because, to some degree or other, we recognise it as coming from outside that person – something given by a 'higher power' or God. And their work also comes to us as a gift. If you have ever found your soul being stirred by music, or your eyes unable to fully take in the beauty of a piece of art, then you will know this unique gift.

There is a long history to gift exchange – it was common in most societies until the introduction of a market economy. And it has been extensively studied by anthropologists in those societies where it still exists.[21] Perhaps the most significant part of this exploration concerns the power dynamics involved in this exchange. To put it bluntly, the obligations involved could be suffocating – the recipient of a gift was expected to give back to the donor – and sometimes the expectations grew and grew.

Hence, Jesus' teaching was radical – give without thinking of a return, give to the ungrateful, give to enemies, and give in secret (Luke 6.35). Saint Paul expands on this as he considers the 'return' as more to do with giving thanks to God, and the right use of the gift. And as John Barclay argues in *Paul and the Gift*[22], since the Greek word charis can be translated either as 'gift' or 'grace', there is a direct link between Paul's emphasis on the grace of God and his teaching about gift giving.

In the next chapter, I will explore how Christians of different cultures and sub-cultures can share and receive gifts. I hope this offers a practical approach to interculturalism, showing how Christians can go beyond a theoretical approach to learning about culture and learning about how individuals and societies respond to different cultures and find a way to grow healthy relationships and even learn to 'love your enemies' (Matthew 5:44).

It is these genuine, human relationships which carry the potential to transform the LLF process.

Questions for reflection

1. What's the most unusual gift you have received? And what's the most unusual gift you have given?

2. Can you think of a time when you have received a gift which has changed the way you think about another person?

3. If Jesus is the greatest gift that anyone can receive, how do we give back to God i.e. return the gift?

3. INTERCULTURALISM AND GIFT EXCHANGE APPLIED TO LLF

To state the obvious, consideration of cultural differences and theological differences is not the same thing. Relating theology and culture is the subject of much discussion in writing on missiology and in the practice of mission (as I said at the beginning of this booklet, this is part of my formative journey and ongoing passion). Cultural encounters can provoke new theological questions and theological understandings. And our deepening theological understandings can provoke new questions about particular expressions of culture.

Sometimes, rather too simplistically, within the LLF process there has been the suggestion that we should celebrate our theological differences (as in multiculturalism). This is not what I am suggesting. This cannot simply be read over from intercultural practice to theology. Nowhere in the Bible are we instructed to 'celebrate different theologies.' Indeed, we could say the opposite – again and again in the New Testament, Paul and the other Apostles warn against false teachers peddling 'a different gospel' (Galatians 1.6). And we are called to 'contend for the faith that was once and for all handed on to the saints.' (Jude v. 3).

Yet it is also true to say that some have approached the LLF process with an 'assimilationist' mindset – if only everybody adopted my approach, everything would be all right! This too bears little resemblance to what we see in the New Testament and early church where we find a rich diversity of approaches to church life. The New Testament scholar James Dunn wrote 'there was no single normative form of Christianity in the first century.'[23] And in fact, much of what we read in the New

Testament is the early church's response to the theological questions raised for them as they took the gospel from 'Jerusalem, [to] all Judea and Samaria, and to the ends of the earth' (Acts 1.8).

The missiologist Andrew Walls refers to this as a process of 'translation'. Indeed he refers to the 'infinite translatability of the Christian faith'.[24] As Christianity crosses cultural boundaries, it encounters 'the burning questions within that culture' and 'the points of reference within it by which people know themselves'. So, Christianity is not bound to a single cultural expression but can directly face and satisfactorily answer the issues of every human culture on earth.

So, I want to be clear that interculturalism does not mean 'anything goes' with regard to theology and doctrine. There are limits to diversity, but defining those limits is a much harder task than many acknowledge. Irenaeus, writing in the second century (he was taught by St Polycarp, who was a disciple of the Apostle John) affirmed the plurality of the four Gospels – Matthew, Mark, Luke and John – each with their different emphases. Irenaeus's most famous book, called *Against Heresies*, makes it very clear that he was concerned for right doctrine, yet his focus in this book is on the incarnation and person of Christ – on this doctrine there is no room for diversity. But on other matters (famously for Irenaeus, the question of the date of Easter) he argued for flexibility.

Despite the divisions within the church that have happened over the centuries, all the major Christian traditions continue to acknowledge the words of the Apostles' Creed and the Nicene Creed. The first is a simple summary of our faith used primarily at baptisms and confirmations. The second is a more detailed statement and was developed in response to the key doctrinal questions faced by the expanding church. Although these questions were specific to the time, there is still general agreement today that matters addressed by the creeds are settled and fixed. These are sometimes referred to as 'first order issues' – something over which we cannot agree to disagree.

Richard Hooker, who is often regarded as the intellectual father of Anglicanism, drew on the distinction between the fundamentals of faith and 'adiaphora' (things indifferent). Where the line is drawn depends on our interpretation of Scripture. Where is the authority of the Bible telling us directly what we should believe and do (in which case our response needs to be obedience)? And where is it providing us with principles and examples which can be applied to situations never envisaged by the authors (in which case we must exercise some judgement of our own)?

This sounds like a neat description. But in practice, the church has often struggled to agree on the distinction.

This is particularly true of LLF. There has been no agreement within the church on what sort of disagreement we are dealing with! Neither marriage nor sex are mentioned in the creeds. There is plenty on both these subjects in the Bible, yet there is much debate on the particular meaning of Greek words and whether the sort of same-sex relationships referred to are the sort of relationships we know today. And marriage in the Old Testament looks very different from that spoken of in the New Testament (e.g. polygamy is accepted in parts of the Old Testament). There are also disagreements about the nature of biblical authority, authorship and inspiration, which arguably, are more fundamental than the specifics of morality.

So, a key question is whether LLF is about fundamentals/ first order issues (definitive to being a Christian) or are they second order issues (important enough that different Christian denominations take different views), or are they third order/ 'adiaphora' (relatively unimportant and not something on which the church should divide)? There is no agreement on the level of disagreement![25]

What then are we to do?

Personally, I believe that the only thing we can do, is to take our time discerning what category of disagreement this constitutes (hence the question 'can we imagine a future together?'), *and* during this time, commit to engaging with one another across difference, i.e. work with the model of interculturalism, and learn how to 'love our enemies' (Matthew 5.44 – arguably a much more fundamental element of what it means to be a follower of Jesus)[26]

This is a season of discernment about both 'what is pleasing to the Lord with regard to identity, sexuality and relationships' and about 'what sort of church are we called to be in 21st Century England?'

In the previous chapter, I suggested that interculturalism requires a process of learning about culture and sub-cultures, about individual and societal responses to difference, and about gift exchange as a practical way to grow relationships across difference. For me, the main thing in common between cultural differences and differences with regard to human sexuality, is the importance of relationships.

The only way forward I see for LLF during this next season is hospitality and gift exchange – practical acts of kindness and generosity which grow relationships and community. This is not to say that we should ignore our theological differences – we must go on addressing them. But we are never going to agree on the theology, so at the same time, let's work on our relationships.

For LLF, this means every church, cathedral, chaplaincy and school committing to grow relationships across difference. And rather than simply seeing this as a slogan, it needs to be translated into concrete action – hence the approach of gift exchange which sees every person as a gift, and every person having gifts to give and to receive.

Such gifts come in all sorts of shapes and sizes – so even if we can't countenance seeing someone else's theology as a gift, we can still see the person as a gift and remain open to the other sort of gifts they may have to give to us and to receive from us. Perhaps in this way, we can find a way to continue to live together.

What does this look like in practice?

To share gifts is to share God's grace. And sharing gifts does not mean that we endorse each other's theology or morality – rather it is a generous and gracious response to the grace and generosity of God. St Paul can write: 'Christ died for us while we were still sinners' (Romans 5.8) implying that our evil acts did not stop God from journeying towards us and interacting with us. Generous giving is in the very nature of God, 'who of thy tender mercy didst give thine only Son Jesus Christ to suffer death upon the Cross for our redemption' (The Book of Common Prayer).

So how might we do this? I think there are three parts to it:

1. **Generous giving**

Can we give without an expectation of return? Can we give to our enemies? This is Jesus' challenge to us. Sadly, we have seen 'giving' used as an expression of power within LLF. Within the Anglican Communion, stories abound of rich Western churches (of different hues) offering 'support' for poorer churches only if they agree to a certain doctrinal position. This is a form of imperialism, and it needs to be named as such. And within the Church of England, there has at times been a similar lack of generosity.

So I want to ask if true generosity would involve supporting churches with whom we disagree? This would be an extraordinary sign of the grace of God, and a 'letting go of power' (since money and power are intricately linked). Giving to those with different views can be done in a way which says, 'we disagree, but we can still love and support each other. '

Of course, the Parish Share/Common Fund is set up to do this, yet it is possible for churches to give over and above their Parish Share with one-off financial gifts!

Similarly, I know of churches which have deliberately organised an exchange of people – from dialogue groups (e.g. a joint LLF course) to ordinands and lay trainees on placement, to invitations to speak. Such exchanges need careful planning to ensure that they are genuinely a safe space for everyone involved. Reflection on the Pastoral Principles is essential, as are agreed 'ground rules' around listening and speaking, use of language, 'time outs', etc.

Further to this, each of us can choose to give our time to people with whom we disagree. Time is precious, and how we choose to spend it is significant. We might also want to explore the gift of tears and the gift of lament – possibly something we can do together as we lament the disunity of the church.

2. **Radical receptiveness**[27]

Can we identify with the other person in a way which enables the saving grace of God to flow between us? Can we receive gifts from someone with whom we disagree profoundly? Can an LGBTQI+ person receive a gift from someone who questions their identity or lifestyle? The answer is yes – I have seen it happen, though I can't imagine how it feels to be in that situation. And similarly, I have seen friendships grow between people with strongly held opposite views on LLF.

Strangely, receiving can be more difficult than giving. (Indeed an African bishop once said to me: 'The problem with the church in the West is that you haven't learnt to receive.')

Radical receptiveness involves remaining open to the power of the gift to change us. But it also involves running the risk of being hurt by the gift. This is why we need brave spaces as well as safe spaces for dialogue and interaction.

Hospitality is key to creating such safe and brave spaces. Eating together offers a powerful way for each person to contribute and receive. It requires careful attention to the needs of the other and helps break down barriers to learning. In the area of cultural differences, preparing and eating food together has been extraordinarily fruitful in bringing people together. Could it also be fruitful for LLF?

3. Transformative thanksgiving

Giving thanks for the gift of God in Christ lies at the heart of Christian worship – Holy Communion, the Eucharist, or The Lord's Supper. Arguably one of the saddest parts of the LLF process has been the unwillingness by some people to share Holy Communion together. This is a tragedy, yet expressive of where we are in this time of discernment. The question, 'Can we imagine a future together?' implies the question 'Can we imagine a time when we will share Holy Communion together?'

With our ecumenical partner churches we can share some communion, but not full communion, so that we don't share the Eucharist with our Roman Catholic friends, yet we still regard them as Christian brothers and sisters. So, a recent document exploring the future of the Anglican Communion (the Nairobi–Cairo Proposals)[28] argues that we are in impaired Communion and can't force each other into a shared table, or rebuke each other for doing so, but at the same time our relationships as Anglicans are more than ecumenical as we share a common story, liturgy, structures, etc.

If we cannot share full communion during this season, how then can we embrace transformative thanksgiving?

I am struck that Paul in his letters often starts by giving thanks for those to whom he is writing, e.g. 1 Corinthians 1.4. And yet, before long, he is challenging and even rebuking the same people in the same letter. Clearly it is possible to give thanks for someone and to disagree with them! And prayer can be a powerful way of holding these things together as God enlarges our hearts and increases our affections (2 Corinthians 6.11–13).

Habits and Attitudes

I believe that our current disagreement will not be settled through one group shouting the loudest, or employing the cleverest arguments, or even by convincing everyone that their interpretation of Scripture is right. For this next season in the life of the church, I suggest that we need to put our energy into the sort of gift exchange shown to us in Christ Jesus:

> who, though he existed in the form of God,
>> did not regard equality with God
>> as something to be grasped,
> but emptied himself,
>> taking the form of a slave,
>> assuming human likeness.

This well-known hymn in Philippians 2 follows on from a plea for humility. This is the 'mind of Christ' which is to shape and form us. And this is the first of a number of habits and attitudes which need to be emphasised in this season of church life.

1. Christ's humility

How can Christ's humility grow within us? Of course, through being united with Christ (Philippians 2.1) and allowing the Holy Spirit to produce fruit within us (Galatians 5.22–23). And the ancient rule of St Benedict contains twelve steps to humility: respect God; love not one's own will; submit to one's superior; be obedient to God at all times, especially in difficult situations; be transparent; be content with lowly and menial jobs; have a correct, but lowly estimation of self; stay within the boundaries of the organisation and role; control one's tongue; avoid frivolity; speak clearly and plainly; adopt a humble posture. I can't help but wonder how different the LLF process would be if we all committed to these twelve steps.[29]

2. **Christ's de-centring**

How do I take myself, my hurt and pain out of the centre so that I can truly listen to the other? This is not about repressing or lying to oneself – we must acknowledge the hurt and pain. But it can't be allowed to shape my whole response to those with whom I disagree.

The Franciscan writer Bonaventure identified Christ's emptying, in poverty, humility and obedience through acts of love, as the one aspect of his life that *all* can imitate. 'We cannot imitate Christ's divine power, his divine wisdom or knowledge,' he said, 'nor can everyone act as a priest at the altar. All can practice self-emptying: the values of poverty, humility and obedience in imitation of Christ. This is the Franciscan path towards holiness! By emptying ourselves in faith we make room for God.'[30]

3. **A child's curiosity**

This may seem an odd choice for a third habit or attitude to emphasise in this context. But it is one of the three formational habits central to the *Difference* course (be curious – be present – reimagine).[31] And it is also central to the intercultural approach outlined in the last chapter. Cultivating curiosity about other cultures and people is key to learning and growth. And it should be no surprise that it is one of the things which children do, which as adults we seem to unlearn! So, the endless questions asked by a small child, which wear out the patience of every parent, are a sign of their desire to learn and understand the world. Might we make a habit of asking questions, seeking understanding and getting to know the person behind the theological position?

Questions for reflection

1. Generous giving. What sort of gifts might you offer to those with whom you disagree?

2. Radical receptiveness. When receiving a gift, you are making yourself vulnerable – it might hurt you. That is a big risk. But equally it might transform your relationship. Can you think of a time when you have made yourself vulnerable and been surprised at the positive outcome?

3. Transformative thanksgiving. If our example is the gift of God in Christ, how might thanksgiving transform our human relationships in the same way that it is the appropriate response to God?

4. Habits and attitudes. What are the habits and attitudes that God is speaking to you about as you read? Are there areas where you need to explore what it means to grow in humility? When and where do you need to be more curious?

4. A LOVE LETTER TO THE CHURCH

> Priests .... share with the Bishop in the oversight of the Church, delighting in its beauty and rejoicing in its well-being.[32]

These are the words that I say every time that I ordain new presbyters in God's church. What does it mean to 'delight' in the beauty and rejoice in the well-being of the church?

Many of us struggle to think of ourselves as beautiful. We compare ourselves endlessly with the 'ideal' with which we are presented in adverts, or among our friends and neighbours. And many of us struggle to think of the Church of England as beautiful. Again, we compare ourselves with other parts of the world, or other denominations, or — even more perniciously — with the ideal that we have in our mind: 'what the church ought to be'. Tragically, we spend a lot of time at General Synod and elsewhere telling each other just how ugly we are as a church, and how person X or group Y is responsible for the decline and divisions of the church. Of course, some of this is justified. The terrible safeguarding failures which have come to light in recent years require real repentance, change and a commitment to ongoing care for victims and survivors. Yet, without in any way downplaying the significance of these failures, they are not the sum total of who we are.

So, what if we dared to believe that God delights in us even while grieving over our sin, our divisions and faithlessness? What if we dared to believe that God looks on us and smiles?

I believe this is possible because I see it in Jesus' encounter with Peter recorded in John 21. Jesus makes no mention of Peter's denial and betrayal, but lovingly re-commissions him: 'Feed my lambs … tend my sheep … feed my sheep … follow me.' This is an example of delighting in someone in full knowledge of their failings. And it takes place in the context of a shared meal.

The International Commission for Anglican Orthodox Dialogue 2006 spoke of the church in these terms:

> By the indwelling grace of the Holy Spirit, the church is created to be an image of the life in communion of the Triune God.[33]

It's a profound statement of our purpose, and it suggests that the model for our common life within the body of Christ is based not on any organisational structure, or hierarchy, but rather the communion that exists between the three persons of the Holy Trinity.

As with Rublev's icon, we are invited to sit and enjoy the communion table with the three persons of the Trinity, each of them sat, heads slightly bowed, expressions of love on their faces. And as we sit, we wonder at the fact that we have been called to join them at that table. And not just us, but all humanity is called to join them at the table, in all our diversity.

The Trinity, Andrei Rublev (early 15th century)

I think we are united in believing that all humanity is invited to the table. I think we are united in believing that we are called to come as we are, to be ourselves and not worry about whether we are wearing the right clothes. I believe we are united in our experience of being changed simply through being sat at the table with the Triune God and listening in to the conversation between the three persons, recorded for us in Holy Scripture. I think we are united in our hope of one day being sat at the table in heaven, and that will be a beautiful sight: 'a great multitude that no one can count, from every nation, from all tribes and peoples and languages' as John says in his vision (Revelation 7.9). I think we can delight in all that unites us.

And now the question is: what are we to do about our divisions – our temporary and fleeting divisions here on earth?

I know that there are some in the Church of England who believe that they can't be in communion with others who have a different view of marriage and sexual ethics.

I don't blame you for wanting the best for God's church. And I want to say to you: you have a place in the Church of England, even if that means the church agreeing to make changes in order to ensure you feel secure within the church. You are loved by God, and God wants you to be sat at the table. And specifically, I say to those who are part of the Alliance,

I know you want to remain in the church. I'm grateful for your commitment to stay part of the dialogue.

Others are willing to stay in communion, but only so long as we don't enshrine injustice in our structures. Again, I don't blame you for wanting the best for God's Church. And I say to you, too: you have a place in the church of England even if that means the church agreeing to make changes in order to ensure you feel secure within the church. You are loved by God, and God wants you to be sat at the table. And specifically, I say to those who are part of the Together network, I know you want to remain in the church. I'm grateful for your commitment to stay part of the dialogue.

We all want the best – and yet we profoundly disagree. So, what now?

What I am offering in this booklet is a middle way between the ideal that we long for, and the reality that we experience. If we place too much emphasis on the former, we will always be disappointed. Too much emphasis on the latter, and we will always be disheartened. So we hold on to hope.

None of wants a world torn apart by wars. None of us wants climate change. None of wants to see people suffer. And yet these are the reality of our world. And rather than giving in to despair, we commit to doing the little we can to make this world a better place, trusting that one day we will see the 'new heaven and new earth' promised by God.

So, in this booklet, I have suggested that 'doing the little we can' involves kindness, generosity, openness (or what I've referred to as receptiveness) and thanksgiving. It's about practical actions which show love in action. And it's about taking this to the extreme of loving our enemies. For this to happen, I've suggested that we need to focus on cultivating particular attitudes – curiosity, humility, and de-centring ourselves. These attitudes are part of what shapes the culture of the church, and we are going to need a lot more of them in this season of our life together.

I am convinced that we all want the best for this beautiful Church of England. Yet I am also convinced that we are going to have to be realistic, knowing that this side of heaven, the church will never be perfect, never be pure, never have true justice. This side of heaven, we must live in hope – longing that one day we will sit together at the table in heaven.

I believe that people across the Church of England want to get on with serving their communities and this nation in the name of Jesus Christ. And it is in doing this – faithfully following Jesus Christ – that we best express what it means to delight in the church. I dare to believe that being generous in giving of ourselves to one another and being radical in receiving the gift we are to one another will lead to a yet unknown but hopeful transformation of our church, enabling us to be thankful and joyful in this mission to which we are all called.

FURTHER RESOURCES

- **Living in Love and Faith resources** (the LLF learning hub, book, course and more) www.churchofengland.org/resources/living-love-and-faith

- **Pastoral Principles** (cards, course and video content) www.churchofengland.org/about/general-synod/structure/house-bishops/pastoral-principles

- **The *Difference* course** difference.rln.global/the-course

- **Learning to pray** www.churchofengland.org/prayer-and-worship/learning-pray

- **Anglican Communion prayers for repentance and reconciliation** www.anglicancommunion.org/media/355990/a-season-of-repentance-en.pdf

- **Intercultural prayer and worship** songs2serve.eu/intercultural-worship-practical-ideas

Endnotes

1   See https://www.churchofengland.org/resources/living-love-and-faith.
2   https://www.churchofengland.org/sites/default/files/2017-11/
gs-2055-marriage-and-same-sex-relationships-after-the-shared-
conversations-a-report-from-the-house-of-bishops.pdf.
3   See https://www.archbishopofcanterbury.org/news/statement-arch
bishop-canterbury-following-todays-general-synod.
4   All the LLF resources can be accessed via: https://www.churchofengland.
org/resources/living-love-and-faith/living-love-and-faith-resources.
5   The Pastoral Principles cards, course and video resources are all available
via: https://www.churchofengland.org/about/general-synod/structure/
house-bishops/pastoral-principles. The cards and course are also available
in print from Church House Publishing via www.chpublishing.co.uk/
livinginloveandfaith.
6   https://www.churchofengland.org/sites/default/files/2022-09/
p1156-coe-living-in-love-faith-findings-report_v8-dps.pdf
7   See www.cofe.io/PrayersOfLoveAndFaith. The initial 2023 version
of the prayers: https://www.churchofengland.org/sites/default/
files/2023-12/prayers-of-love-and-faith.pdf. A bespoke (or standalone)
service is 'a service of Public Worship organised explicitly to pray to
God with a same-sex couple that would not have taken place otherwise'.
8   https://togethercofe.org.uk/9 https://alliancecofe.org/
9   https://alliancecofe.org/
10 The Declaration of Assent, see: *To Proclaim Afresh: Declarations and
Oaths for Church of England Ministers*, Faith and Order Commission,
Church House Publishing, 2022, p. 1: https://www.churchofengland.
org/sites/default/files/2022-06/PROCLAIMtextWEB.pdf.
11 As I explore later in this booklet (p. 29 onwards), culture has a direct
effect on how we do theology, ethics, missiology and ecclesiology, as well
as how we view our identity and relationships.
12 Ronald A. Heifetz, *Leadership without Easy Answers*, Harvard University Press, 1994.
13 See Margaret O'Gara, *Receiving Gifts in Ecumenical Dialogue* in Paul Murray (Ed),
*Receptive Ecumenism and the Call to Catholic Learning: Exploring a Way for Contemporary
Ecumenism*, OUP, 2009.
14 https://www.churchofengland.org/about/general-synod/structure/
housebishops/pastoral-principles
15 See the also the LLF document *Braver and Safer: Creating spaces for learning together
well:* https://www.churchofengland.org/media/38431
16 Source: https://www.americanbar.org/news/profile-legal-profession/
demographics.

17   See: https://www.churchofengland.org/sites/default/files/2018-
     01/gsmisc-1171-discerning-in-obedience-report-on-the-review-of-
     the-cnc.pdf, pp. 5-6.
18   https://www.psephizo.com/sexuality-2/does-gods-widening-mercy-
     contradictbiblical-sexual-ethics/?fbclid=IwY2xjawGR1atleHRuA2Flb
     QIxMQABHZ9PPj1K2JENR5AKlu6mGAUYWZQrBLwX80djY-
     6yblIDdD05W8A4wO1pw_aem_p5CkAyvsxpHWWaZsJkzutw
19   https://mbarrattdavie.wordpress.com/2024/09/30/1805/
20   Gullahorn, J. E., & Gullahorn, J. T. (1963), 'An Extension of
     the U-CurveHypothesis,' *Journal of Social Issues* 19, 33–47.
21   See *An Intercultural Church for a MulticulturalWorld* (CHP, 2024)
     for a fuller exploration of this literature and history.
22   John M. G. Barclay, *Paul and the Gift*, Eerdmans, 2015.
23   James D. G. Dunn, *Unity and Diversity in the New Testament, an Enquiry
     into the Character of Early Christianity*, SCM, 2005
24   Andrew Walls, *The Missionary Movement in Christian History:Studies in the
     Transmission of the Faith*, Orbis Books, 1996.
25   For more on this, see https://www.churchofengland.org/sites/default/files/
     2017-10/communion_and_disagreement_faoc_report_gs_misc_1139.pdf.
26   See Dr Martyn Lloyd-Jones, *Studies in the Sermon on the Mount*, who describes
     Matthew 5-7 as "the clearest description of what Christians are meant to be".
27   Please note, I am using the word 'receptiveness' to distinguish this from
     'receptivity' which carries a formal, technical sense in theology. So I am
     referring here very simply to being open to receiving gifts from others.
28   See: https://www.anglicannews.org/news/2024/12/iascufo-
     paper-explores-anglican-communion-identity-and-vocation.aspx.
29   For an example of how these twelve steps might apply today, see:
     https://www.regent.edu/journal/inner-resources-for-leaders/rule-of-st-
     benedict-12-steps-of-humility-in-leadership and Augustine Wetta, *Humility
     Rules: Saint Benedict's Twelve-Step Guide to Genuine Self-Esteem*, Ignatius Press, 2017.
30   Taken from Ilia Delio, *Simply Bonaventure:An Introduction into his Life, Thought
     and Writings*, New City Press, 2001. See also Helen Julian, *Franciscan Footprints:
     Following Christ in the ways of Francis and Clare*, BRF, 2020.
31   https://difference.rln.global/the-course/
32   The Ordination of Priests, also called Presbyters, *Common Worship Ordination
     Services* https://www.churchofengland.org/prayer-and-worship/worship-
     texts-and-resources/common-worship/ministry/common-worship
     ordination-0.
33   https://www.anglicancommunion.org/media/103818/The-Church-of-
     the-Triune-God.pd